Blessings,

Lauren
Chagnon

ISBN: 9798779203319

Imprint: Independently published

Published by Civin Media Relations

www.civinmediarelations.com

Printed in the United States

Table of Contents

~ Introduction ~

Laura Chagnon began publishing poetry in 2014 with a very successful first book, "Never Touched a Pen." Laura is not able to write poetic words or use a computer. She has never seen any of the 6,000 plus poems she created in print. You see, Laura is quadriplegic and legally blind. Add to that, a traumatic brain injury that challenges her short-term memory. Overcoming these obstacles is a testament to the strength of the human spirit. The fact that Laura never makes excuses or seeks pity of any kind shows an unbreakable demeanor.

A senseless assault on her 26th birthday in 1989 caused several adversities. Surviving that near-death experience changed her life, Laura became a born-again Christian. She felt an extreme closeness to God, which she still feels to this day and that was a major step in coping with disabilities. Her poetry covers a wide range, it can be spiritual, the love of nature and also being very open about physical challenges.

Being extremely modest and humble should not detract from the pride Laura gained in all that she has accomplished. Laura lets the many followers judge the quality of her work. It would be quite a challenge to find a more inspirational poet in America. Laura's goal is to continue writing poetry that will touch the hearts of those who read her works. She sets a very high standard for writing poetry, Laura is very much a perfectionist. She is most at peace when God lovingly whispers in her ear, a warm breeze caresses her soul and the music of birds fills the air as she creates another beautiful poem.

Here is a collection of Laura Chagnon's best works.

~ Dedication ~

I would like to first lovingly dedicate this book to God. He saved my life when death seemed imminent after a brutal assault. My eyes opened to His love for me which continues each and every day.

Next, my parents Wayne and Carole for their unconditional love. Without their tireless dedication, I would not be able to live with the hope I feel in my heart.

I want to thank Pastor Jack Desroches for his love and spiritual guidance. His beautiful faith in God is a shining example which I treasure.

My friend and publisher, Todd Civin, has helped me realize my dreams. Poetry is the gift I possess and Todd has opened that gift to others.

Finally, I dedicate this book to my soulmate, Tom. I would say he has pulled me along for the last 21 years, but to be accurate, Tom has pushed my wheelchair with dedication and love. My life with him is filled with abundant joy.

~ Me ~

I'm the woman in bed
but it's not really me,
I'm the gulls in the sky
soaring over the sea.

I'm a colorful butterfly
when I pretend,
as I drift through the summer
I'm everyone's friend.

On the limb of a beech tree
in sparkling weather,
I'm the wings of a cardinal
with my red feathers.

I emerge from my dreams
in the first light of dawn,
I'm an angel in heaven
white as a swan.

These visions of freedom
are my soul's gift to me,
I'm a peaceful poet
my words set me free.

~ Bite of the Apple ~

I'll always believe in you

each ripple of wave

each flower petal

each wing of bee and bird.

I'll always believe in you

eyes wide, filled with innocence.

Until your eyes become hard as sidewalks

until you take a bite of the apple.

When you tell your first lie

when you become human.

~ A Tribute to Creation ~

I feel you most when I look at the sky.
I imagine a face, a cloud always changing.
How can I question when the table is set?

Before twilight, goblets of wine gracefully topple
with a push of invisible hands.

There is an outline, porcelain white.
A teapot pouring the moon from its spout—
pouring the stars, the planets.

And in this sky, embroidered with stars, I feel you most,
warm eyes of summer days.

~ Coma ~

My sleep was long
emerging from the outstretched arms of death.
The train departs, and I'm the only passenger
left behind inside the station.

A picture always out of focus,
looking at the world through black spider webs,
communication--
like searching for lost puzzle pieces.

From a darkened cavern, I grasp onto thoughts,
but they drift in and out of the fog, then slither
away, like mercury from a broken thermometer.

This can't be me, this package of skin and bones
hearing voices without faces,
unable to move--So much fear!

Surrounded by strangers in this dark world,
spiraling down, down,
my head spinning with confusion.

Falling off the earth, cold waves wash over me,
imprisoned by my body
and the pain, the endless pain.

I pray that my old self will slip back inside
this body, like a transparent apparition,
and together we will disappear
where no pain can follow us.

A familiar voice pulls me from my shadow land.
I hear my stranger's voice
tears slide down my face
I'm still here!

~ Kind People ~

The quick flash of a camera
taking the perfect picture.
Sometimes she felt strong and thought
she could gallop with the wild horses
and mingle with the hungry herd.

Eye to eye she would look courageously
into each face, her heart would not quiver,
her words would glisten, like silver rivers
rushing over polished stones.

If this dream came true, she could dance among
the stars in another galaxy. If this dream came true,
she would no longer live in alienation
with the few kind people of the world.

For a moment, she could drink their wine
and live inside their social caves.
But when the stars begin to fall in the stormy fire,
she will be on the island,
watching the world disappear into the sea,
a leader of a small band of kind people.

~ Eternity ~

Our hearts drop
like seeds into the soil of our flesh.
Captured in moonlight,
millions of feathers silently fall
to a place of dreams.

If we tear past the burrows,
a sky opens up, and we feel the wind,
and the wings of two hawks
gliding in a silver breeze.

A mountain's peak beyond the clouds,
trees grow from the garden of our hearts,
housing the spirits of the wind.

One by one we flock
to branches made of bone.
Our thoughts are simply understood,
the brilliant air is filled with song,
and the unspeakable cold has disappeared.

From the tips of branches,
from the ledge of the universe,
wings touching wings, for all eternity.

~ With Every Rose a Thorn ~

If your eyes are flowers and you bend

at the stem, if your scent is too sweet,

never will you thrive in this

box of nails, standing eye to eye

with hammers driven into walls.

You'll always live, sweet-tasting, devoured,

but your mouth holds sharp fangs,

too shy for the taste of bitter grapes.

~ New Fallen Snow ~

You're the flower, you're the flame,

face that lights my face. You spin intelligence

into these particles that I am.

Your wind shivers my tree. My mouth tastes sweet with your

name on it.

You make my dance daring enough to finish.

No more timidity!

Let fruit fall and wind turn my roots up in the air. Rain has felt

its last tear drop, those cold pupils.

I see my reflection in the topaz.

In your arms, I am a glass swan, fragile,

yet I feel passion glow in the pools of your eyes.

I feel the excited flutter, jeweled cascades, white butterflies of

new fallen snow. Enough for now to be here, content in the dove's

hypnotic coo.

~ I the River ~

I am water, always rushing,

my spirit is the river,

ceaselessly hurrying but never tire.

I am God's beloved

and sense Him everywhere.

I am home for many living beings

and quench the thirst of man and beast.

My body polishes stones in my wake.

So grateful to my Creator,

my banks are rich with life.

I feel the little feet

of many creatures scurry by.

I experience the doe drinking water,

my own heart thrilled to satisfy her appetite.

I hear the voice of people,

their souls so content as they fish,

as I listen to the reel of poles casting out into my home

and perceive the sensation of adrenaline.

All the while,

sorrow,

deep sorrow,

as one of my children will lose the fight of life.

I the river,

gazing skyward,

so delighted to watch the passing clouds.

I am ecstatic,

so ecstatic,

for the privilege and the honor

to be alive.

~ Heaven ~

Come listen to the lullaby of water
right down here by the sacred stream,
fall asleep in my wings now child
and feel the most beautiful dream.

This is the village of paradise
where all the birds perch to sing,
come my child let me take your hand
and soar with your new gentle wings.

This is a place called home
a place where there is no fear,
listen to the heartbeat of angels
can you feel all the love right here?

Let tranquility shine in your eyes now
feel the warmth of my radiant sun,
relax in the arms of paradise
for now you are forever young.

You are the lamb in my arms now
let tears of happiness flow,
you are safe here for eternity
and my arms will never let go.

There are no computers or fast cars
or material things, just to be,
all you need is faith in your heart
in a vision so beautiful to see.

Come listen to the lullaby of water
right down here by the sacred stream,
fall asleep in my wings now child
and feel the most beautiful dream.

~ *A Message to Cancer* ~

When you first came around I loathed you
but I didn't want to be that rash,
so the light of my spirit wouldn't dampen
so the light of my spirit wouldn't crash.

We live together never peacefully
not ever will I call you friend,
to my life you bring nothing but sorrow
and my journey you threaten to end.

There is not one thing gracious about you
to give in I'd never be willing,
so quickly you've crept into my life
a dark and most ominous villain.

My aspiration in life to abolish you
all the despair and anguish you give,
but with the power of God and His love
He grants me the grace to live.

Dear sweet Lord in heaven
I'm so grateful for all that you do,
I hold up my candle in tribute
for the elegance that can only be you.

~ *Crows of Late August* ~

Crickets, crickets, crickets, I love their wild happiness.
Their glorious voices serenading in the oracle of
shadows in this late summer dream.
But that is not what this poem is about,
let's take several footsteps backwards.

On the deck where I peacefully perch beneath the afternoon sun,
the last day of August, much quieter are the birds now.
Many have packed their feathers and flown south.
My heart delighted when I hear the majestic crows,
their voices quarreling in this late summer's sky.

Today the colors on the trees still verdant,
the very tips of leaves dipped in crimson.
My spirit is fatigued as I bid farewell to
August in the early September sky.
Blank pages of a new chapter, anxiously
waiting for my pen to baptize their creation.

~ Detour ~

I feel the excited heartbeat of life awakening.

The flame of passion that will not be kept,

the short green mile before the road detours,

turning a corner all too soon to another season.

Seven white butterflies, I watched you dance,

your brief audition upon a yellow ribbon.

And now inside the jar, the glowing flower dies.

Leaves build a patio on the floor--cold castles bend,

turn, twist in the wind--and the sun--the cradle,

an old man now, lost in the vulnerable sky.

Taking that trip back too soon,

we have just shaken the dead mouse from our wings,

stuffed fat with memories in the cat's mouth

dropped at my doorstep. I feel life's shiver

in my palm, the ecstasy of brilliant stars

as I wait, rocking, rocking, as I wait.

~ If I Could Stop Time ~

There is a crystal ball that is my soul,

earth spinning ahead.

Spinning ahead,

the acrobat walks the tightrope,

slipping, falling in snow.

As I walk through a sea

of leaves, I look at the trees' bony limbs,

and those remaining.

In my own marrow,

I feel their sorrow, unable to sail.

I love what I will always love,

eyes that caress the sky,

eyes that stay open,

until the moon rises to the serenade

of crickets, clutching green leaves

in their dreams.

~ Broken Wings ~

I never really examined what has happened to me.

Life, a face in the mirror, too ugly to confront.

I look the other way, a prisoner in my bed.

I gaze outside my window, my window, my window.

There is always my window.

If I look across the street beyond my neighbor's house, a snow-
covered mountain blends into the sky, white then grey.

Solitude can be peaceful; solitude can be lonely like the lonely
white fields after the storm.

A red cardinal brightens the grey with his feathers.

Such is life when you have fallen from grace.

I am a bird with broken wings crashing to the ground.

But today, I have learned to soar.

~ Bone Orchard ~

I feel the night falling, crimson mirror, broken.

Through my window you beckon me, my beloved friend,

Siamese twin, my anxious heart, black bat

cloaked in funeral garb.

There is a plate of blue porcelain, the sky I yearn for.

Was it your spirit I felt as I screamed into this world?

This conception, curse or blessing?

I peer into open mouth, new grave.

I smell the scent of your perfume, fresh spill,

as the turnstile spins, I feel the darkness of torment.

Was it your spirit I felt as I screamed into this world?

This conception, curse or blessing?

~ *The Rooster and the Wristwatch* ~

From the lungs of the rooster shouts time,

a curt reminder of the ticking clock.

Music drifts through the flute,

as bees pollinate the caves of sweet roses.

What I wish to be is this:

perfection of time on pause. . .

but the rooster holds

the watch, shouts time,

a curt reminder of the ticking clock.

~ Crystal Swan ~

From my window heaven has lowered its wrought iron gates.
Hazel eyes, cold tears falling, drops of rain singed by the raven's
broken nest.

Suspended in time, one lonely virgin crying for help,
cold dark fire singeing her wings.
Lost ghost burning with grief, the road never ends.

Soon she hears the echo, God's voice calling from the paradise of
heaven, calling her back.

Tomorrows are forbidden dreams, dreams forbidden.
A gift thrown down from God, this lovely dainty bird whose tears
fall in the dust, her footprints scalded there as she walks to the
shadows, as she walks to the gates of Eden.

~ Captured in the Fire ~

Sparrows fly beyond blades of grass.
I live behind the clouds
and stand humbly in the corner of the sky.

The sun's rays pierce like golden arrows.
A raucous caw dwells deep inside my head,
sharp claws picking me apart,
trailing bits and pieces of my soul.

Clouds pass by, leaving me alone and paralyzed,
to watch a world in motion.

A speck of sunlight spirals shadows across my chair,
wheels of fire captured in the crimson close of day,
as I watch the sparrows fly away.

~ Flying ~

For the joy of it. . .

Imagine being someone other

than yourself for just one day.

Instead of a sweater, grab a pair of wings

from your ordinary closet.

Cancel all plans and practice flying.

Feel the magic in your bones--

Search for the open window, and remember,

it's your presence that paints the gray sky blue.

~ The Seven Angels of Certainty ~

Once upon a beautiful,

lovely spring day.

Seven angels sent from heaven,

with a message to convey.

The first angel was the sun

a little dizzy from her flight.

In her brilliant, golden wings,

she held the dazzling light.

The second angel was rain,

quenching the earth with showers.

The third angel planted seeds,

for fragrant, glorious flowers.

The fourth angel is hope,

dancing with beautiful style.

Summer dreams are breathtaking,

here for a long while.

My heart is so content

in this glorious month of May.

For all my summer angels

are finally on their way.

The fifth angel was the robin,

love carried upon her wings.

The sixth angel is the melody

that every bird will sing.

Let's not forget the butterflies,

with a message of their own.

Perched upon a summer rose

an ornament to call home.

Once upon a beautiful,

lovely summer day.

Seven angels sent from heaven,

forever here to stay.

~ Four Seasons ~

As the last mountain of snow melts,

I bid farewell to winter, with the sweet taste

of a season changing upon my breath.

It begins with a seed, hope's seed, so simple, so lovely.

It is the season of spring. In this time of promise,

we welcome all infants. All trees hold out their arms

to them, as tiny buds begin their blossoming.

This breathtaking lady tending the flowers,

from her bountiful garden.

Born into light, the arrival of summer.

Summer, elegant lady, holds the golden sun.

I stand beneath her, my own heart calm,

my limbs languid from the warmth of her brilliant shine.

I bathe in ecstasy in this house of light,

the hand of summer holding the lantern high

through endless days of harmony. So many wonders

to behold. My spirit enthralled with the first

cricket's song. And the harmonious ballad

of my darling cicadas.

And of course, always the precious birds,
each with a glorious song of their own.

The fires have been blazing all summer,
waiting for the hand of autumn to carry the message along.
Beautiful, Lady of Fall, with her auburn hair, lighting the trees,
each leaf with the flame of her fire.
So breathtaking, she is beautiful to behold before the falling.
Her elegant hands letting go with the essence of her spirit,
carpeting the ground with color.
The season of winter, so regal, so brave, her noble heart
comfortable in its emptiness. For months she stands alone, frigid
winds her only song. Castles of ice glisten in the sun. Ah, the first
snow, so dazzling, cascading diamonds, butterflies in white. It
seems the whole world holds its breath as it silently falls.

Four seasons, winter, spring, summer, fall, each one a child of
God, blessed with an angel's heart.

~ A Lifetime in a Single Flower ~

Isn't life so like a flower?

It begins with a seed, love's seed
deep in God's most generous soil.

Each one blossoms with the purity of God's love.

In dawn's sweet, early light I emerge
confident with a strong spine,
sunshine drops its blessings on me.

When I take my first breath,
faith lives within my soul
and the dream begins.

I'm the child of spring,
my petals first blossoming,
my head tilted towards the sky
watching the beauty of clouds drift by.

The harmony of my spirit bedazzled in
sunlight's warming grace.

I feel all of life's passions deep in

the depths of my roots,

as everything moves around me exchanging a kiss with

a butterfly's wish.

I am in love with this life

everything it offers.

When I'm thirsty I drink the rain,

my hunger subsided every day as

I bring glory to admiring eyes.

I give back to the Lord my

gift of life when the bees

drink my nectar,

from flower to flower I am born

again and again.

So content are my roots

I never tire of this world,

for every day I am maturing as

seasons change, growing old with the summer,

growing wiser with each passing hour.

My arms reaching out

dancing in the moon's embrace,

in the waking of its first hour

the ghost of itself, a pale silhouette.

My petals tremble with joy

as I celebrate the summer.

Time passes slowly, passes quickly,

then at last I take my final breath

in the hour of midnight,

in the birth of autumn's glory, in the wake of summer's death.

~ Raven's Blood ~

Every day, every season, I hear you my beloved.

In the blessing of spring, in the oasis of

winter, always you--your voice a double-drum of confidence.

A piercing arrow through September skies,

your language, a hurricane of noble words,

a sentinel to every gate of every season,

so bold in your uniform of black feathers.

On the ground, in the air, you are always there.

I want to be one with you, my hero.

My heart is yours. So I dip my quill in raven's blood,

etch feathers on my skin, a single plume behind my ear.

In the blaze of autumn, I pause for a moment.

The time has come for me to leave the stage.

In a language only you would understand,

I bid farewell to you, my brother. I dance here in the shadow talk

of your glossy wings,

awaiting your raucous call to carry me home.

~ Fast Sneakers ~

Time vanishes like magic,
like the missing sock, it disappears.
Where does it go?

All day long we work,
seconds run away on fast sneakers.
Time flies on quick wings,
like birds soaring through the clouds.

We want to spend time with our children,
take long walks in the park,
but time walks away.

The shadows are growing, seasons change,
our children say good-bye,
we wake up to grandchildren.

Sand rushes through the hourglass.
The ghost moon rises, a silver phantom,
floating through night.

Night rolls up its dark skirt,
and slips away in a dream.
Morning sun rises, a white dove,
and slips away in a dream, in a heartbeat.

~ Statuesque ~

The clouds are elusive

always slipping from her hands,

they are never hers to own.

She is a statue now

her chiseled face stares out a broken window,

spiders crochet a web above her head.

The museum is an illusion

a real heart beats within her breast,

this is the sound she hears within her dream.

She wears the avalanche of night

like a satin gown--her only jewelry

a tiny pearl, the teardrop in her eye.

Her marble skin can't breathe,

she begs to awaken.

~ The Dark and Light of Things ~

As the dark and light of things

play tug of war, I have questions.

With my thimble full of faith,

how can I believe such invisible threads?

Without a needle, how can I sew

a web of faith and keep the spiders

of disbelief from making a question mark?

A question mark so big it blocks

the entrance to heaven.

That was yesterday's darkness,

it took years for the blindfold to be removed,

to feel His presence,

my faith discovered by heaven's golden rays.

~ The Birth of Twilight ~

Overhead, a gathering of clouds
white as angel wings.
Light breeze dancing through my hair.
It's the time of day that ponders...
that ponders, what shall I do?

It's as if God heard the question,
and answered with a soft veil of twilight
whispering from His lips.

The birds rejoice
celebrating the moment with a song.

This time of day I cherish, so special,
like a long-awaited holiday.

So bewitching is the sky,
a glorious runway of blue that never
ceases to amaze me.

The angel of dusk balancing time
upon her lavender wings.
Outside in God's miraculous kingdom, every moment,
my spirit is enthralled.

Upon this hour, a gathering of mystical shadows,
the birds too are mesmerized,
within their hearts a spell is cast.
Upon their voices so many excited notes
waltzing in enthusiastic circles.

I hear the constant twittering of this bird, of that bird.
Their wings in continuous motion
flooded with new-fledged blossoms on every tree.

The sketch of the moon claims its home--
every early eve it seems to be in the same place.
I, chosen by the Lord, readily accepted,
become a sentinel of this phenomenon called life.

~ Escape ~

They thrived on his anguish,

like predators with cold eyes,

like sharks beneath the water

in a feeding frenzy.

Where was the sun?

Every day there was rain

and every day there was fear.

In his dreams there were fences,

he was trapped inside.

He was the wind,

a wild horse running free.

Tomorrow, the crows will come

picking at his sorrow.

He didn't understand

the direction of life,

the fuel that it took to hate.

Fear built a wall between two worlds.

They pulled him from water's broken mirror.

From the water, he enters into light.

Today, in that dark world,

the sun will shine without him.

~ Where Angels Come to Sing ~

Through the gates of Eden
a harmony of voices.
In the flower bed, a paradise where
angels come to sing.

Overhead are many clouds
blissfully drifting on a pallet of blue.
In this kingdom I sense God's grace everywhere.
In my own heart I feel the Lord's drum
peacefully beating in rhythm with heaven's gentle wind.

I am so blessed when I hear
the ballad of many birds.
Or could this be paradise
where angels come to sing?

~ Crows of Late Autumn ~

Outside inhaling autumn's sweet scent,

rustic.....inviting.

Sunlight shimmering through a lacy

curtain of clouds.

It's October. I'm content in

the cozy shadows of this

comfortable den. Overhead, the

horizon, irresistible as always.

I never met a sunset I have

not fallen completely in love with.

This day's sky, gift-wrapped in

the finest of cloth. White clouds

of sheer satin bliss.

Perched in a tree, a guardian,

a presence in black.

My beloved crow. His voice

greeting me with confident laughter.

Fingers of a chilly wind

strumming the chimes as the

strong breeze rustles through the leaves.

Fallen soldiers red, yellow, gold, copper

somberly drifting in our little pond.

And always the harmonious crows.

Their magical voices calling my name.

~ Crows in Company ~

A crow, black as depression, clings to a branch.

In this wild world, another vagabond crow searching for food.

A sparrow perched on a piano stool is singing the blues,

a pigeon drunk on berries, her fat body can barely fly.

I see them every day, winged soldiers, reminding me of humans,

fighting to survive.

~ Best Friends ~

From the heavens, this sacred gift, our friendship.

Two autumn leaves, vibrant, our spirits together intertwining.

A world so vast, the wind, the clouds, always moving.

And, of course, our friendship,

there are no harsh storms or sharp edges, just serenity,

the gentle wind drifting, drifting.

~ Reborn ~

Deep in earth's most sacred soil
a seed is planted.
And from the seed the most gentle of risings,
everywhere, flowers posed on slender stems.
God's precious emeralds blossoming on the branch,
within this emerald, a trembling of new life waking; ecstatic joy.
And on this Easter day
the most breathtaking of all miracles,
a vision to behold.
With great jubilation we celebrate the Messiah,
the day of His rebirth,
the grace of eternal hope,
the resurrection of the most miraculous phenomenon.
Spreading His arms offering His love to the world,
it's a rainbow of the holiest light,
the most exquisite glow.....Christ reborn.

~ More Than a Job ~

My tears are specks of dust falling, my body is a factory.

My heart is a time clock, you punch in, you punch out.

In the corners of my soul are the shadows of despair,

I am not a bolt to be sorted or a piece of material to be sewn.

I am flesh and blood, my feelings are tender,

please treat me like a person.

I understand your financial burdens.

I understand your need to survive.

You don't look back at the end of the day, your wings open

and soar as you fly away.

The prison of my body is the factory where you work.

I am here forever, forever I am here.

~ Two Lives ~

Freedom is laughter.

Freedom is jumping out of bed,

as easy as the wind

whispers through leaves.

My life as it was,

lingers in the back room,

in the mirror of my memory.

I was walking from room to room,

running upstairs,

running downstairs.

My legs had wings,

I felt my flesh and bones,

my arms and legs were real.

My life as it is, unyielding.

In glass windows,

my face is the same.

But my legs have forgotten

what freedom is--

prisoners of limitations.

Birds fly--

their wings in rapid movement,

as easy as the wind

whispers through leaves.

Like a fly stuck to paper, I am here forever.

My legs are like petrified limbs of trees,

I feel them turn to stone.

~ A New England Picture ~

At the Summer House, children everywhere, eating ice cream,

their small round faces aglow, laughing, squealing,

bringing me to life.

A family circle, a father talking, proud rooster,

mother and daughter leaning in

with listening ears.

Early evening, seashell, coral sunset,

summer breeze gently caressing my face,

serenity.

In the distance, a steeple peeks through lavender clouds,

a small, white church framed with tree tops, their leaves still
green,

noble sentinels captured in the tranquil sky.

In this moment, hope speaks quietly,

"Lay down your swords, let peace

be the shine upon the window of your heart."

~ All Things Bright and Beautiful ~

"Listen closely."

said a whisper in the wind.....

"Do you hear the turning of the key"?

The Lord proposed a toast to the coming season.

Soon everywhere, the door to spring will be opening.

"Cheers!" exclaimed the daffodils in a dignified air.

Look over there at the forsythia,

always the first to blossom,

like tiny drops of sunshine awakening.

Their hearts overflowing with excited giggles.

Let me invite you to gaze upon the tulips,

the epitome of spring.

Balancing colorful cups atop their tall and regal stems.

"Pick me! Pick me!" declared the glorious dandelions.

Their jubilant roars heard in backyards near and far.

I'm looking forward to the first day,

that friendly moment of warmth,

the shine of the sun a treasured gift.

Its golden rays embrace the world

with a miraculous soothing touch.

~ Destiny ~

Yesterday the sun did shine,
though it didn't illuminate my heart.
In my soul, broken light,
my footsteps in darkness,
shambling down the wrong path.

My faith, a dim star, uneasy, always in question,
always alone, no true love to call my own.
The sky overhead fraught with clouds,
every day sharp spears, cruel rain.

Then one day lightning struck,
the last rung in my ladder, splintered,
as I collided with fate.

God caught me in His arms and gave me wings to soar.
My sight has been lost, but God has blessed me
with the greatest of gifts,
a glorious opportunity to envision life poetically,
and the passion to share it with the world.

The footsteps of time are in motion,
but my own footsteps are forever motionless.
The path I now travel is trimmed with flowers
and overhead a brilliant sky is lit with stars.

Though I'll never again stand
and feel the earth beneath my feet, acceptance.
For my spirit has carried me to places
my feet could never travel.
Forever I will soar
with the power of God's flame
burning within my heart.

No more questions, only answers,
blossoms flourishing with faith.
God has blessed me with the strength
to believe,
vision to create,
and a spirit at peace.

~ Moonlight Over Manhattan ~

I am the moon,
my regal shine beaming over Manhattan,
a sentinel of the Lord sent here to guide this fascinating empire.

I am a pigeon,
perched upon a bench in Central Park,
it is another marvelous day here in the city.

I am the nanny,
pushing a carriage with a precious jewel
peeking out from an array of blankets,
a beloved pampered princess in her silky bonnet,
thrilled to be alive in her brand new world.

I am a drifter,
no permanent roots to call home,
a soldier of poverty,
my thoughts every day to merely survive.

I am the lady of the night,
I stroll the West Side, the East Side,
my feet high off the ground in stilettos,
wearing a mask of insincere smiles.

I am a fifteen-year-old runaway,
my heart desperate,
tangled in the spider web lost and broken,
unable to go back home.

I am an actress,
no longer struggling,
my name in brilliant lights flashing on Broadway,
my spirit high on fame, on drugs.

I am a young executive,
gazing out the window of my penthouse,
my heart has grown cold and callous as cement.

I am the worker,
pouring cement,
building another high-rise,
the jackhammer and I are one,
fully empowered,
sweat trickles beneath my hard hat.

I am the cab driver,
who brought his family over from India,
no longer penniless,
living the dream.

I am a thief,
without a conscience,
remembering a childhood,
every day a storm of pelting rain.

I am a native New Yorker,
my spirit filled with grit and pride,
every day taking another bite of the Big Apple.

I am the Statue of Liberty
standing tall and regal,
my torch's flame is powerful
welcoming all who journey here.

~ Alone ~

No place for sensitive emotions,

when a school bell rings

and a child cries inside.

Fear locked behind a face of stone,

masquerading a lost soul.

No place in the schoolyard

for the quiet ones,

so they flock together

in their guarded circle,

letting down their shield

only with each other.

Years later they will search

for a soul mate to build a family,

then try to shed away

youthful fears, like a snakeskin,

to find a place to fit.

They will lick the wounds

of yesterday, adjusting the mask

to adulthood, to walk along

the crowded footpath

to the ultimate reality--we are not alone.

~ Roses ~

From the lavender pool of night,

dreams are the color

of fog in early morning.

In this life, the colors are gray.

I watch my rabbit,

white as snow,

her tiny, pink eyes full of fear,

as she trembles in the cage.

Into solitary heaven,

I escape when the black tongues

whisper in the poisonous cave.

Here, my colors shine,

like a brand new penny

or a polished kettle.

I never was a rose

or a brilliant feather

in a garden of friends.

I would have flourished

on a smaller planet

where the winds were kind.

Overnight, my petals

would have blossomed.

Each morning,

in the alien sun,

I would wake in this strange garden,

where every flower was a rose.

~ And Sparrow Takes a Bath ~

We've taken many footsteps down summer's path

and, like a beloved toy, no longer new,

that shine has worn off a bit.

But the birds don't seem to notice,

every morning they wake with a song in

their hearts.

Never selfish, performing in summer's

theatre from the light of dawn until day's end,

sharing their joy.

When I see the darling faces of the sparrows,

I think of angels. And today, this day,

one of my angels is taking a bath in our little pond,

the pond my father built--

frolicking, baptizing himself in God's sweet water.

And in this moment, I felt my heart stir, and realized

how fragile life is, how thoroughly amazing it is.

For aren't we all like this little sparrow,

our bodies so delicate, fragile, but strong in spirit,

sharing our song with the world.

~ When Passion Speaks ~

When passion speaks:
I am writing about all the things I so adore,
cruising on the vessel of thoughts.

Passion speaks:
When I am outside,
so peaceful is my spirit
when I gaze skyward into an ocean of blue.

God's gifts surround me,
they are everywhere,
in a flower, in the leaves of all the trees,
so noble and amazing.

His gifts reach out to cicadas,
blessing their hearts with a harmonious song.
I'll not forget the crickets,
whose melody frolics in the wind,
spring, summer and fall.

Passion speaks:
This autumn eve,
as my soulmate and I share a kiss,
as geese fly by in the moonlight.

Passion speaks:
It is winter,
so much beauty everywhere.
Especially the trees,
breathtaking in their emptiness,
hands open collecting crystal jewels from angels.

Passion speaks:
In the silence of snow falling
ever so quietly from God's house,
His heavenly kingdom far above.

Passion speaks:
From the heart of our pastor,
quite harmoniously,
as he delivers the sermon every Sabbath day.

When passion speaks:
To my soul on so many occasions,
in so many glorious ways.

~ The Fisherman ~

The storm held them in dark confusion.

The sea poured its harsh fury into the ship,

sinking, sinking. . ..

grief buried beneath turquoise waves.

Noble were the waters they set sail upon that day--the fisherman's spirit, joyful as the wild waves, independent as the sea birds overhead.

Seagulls glide above the lighthouse, above the buoys. Families gather at the dock, peering down into hell, at the bottomless ocean that swallowed their love, their world.

In another era, divers discovered the boat

and the forgotten bones of the fisherman,

grief buried beneath turquoise waves.

~ Gratitude ~

Every morning I give thanks when I wake,
as the pink rays of dawn lift me up,
greet me at my bedroom window.

I am grateful, grateful to the wind and sky,
hawk and crow soaring by.

Every spring our wealthy land
gives birth to promise
and crops grow high in fields of splendor.
The angel of gratitude
soars upon wings of serenity,
her heart filled with hope.

The golden wealth of summer,
offering its warm embrace.
The scarlet tears of fall
passionately follows.

On Thanksgiving, the cornucopia
decorates the festive table.
The sun, a gracious troubadour,
offering tranquility to every heart.

~ Forgotten Fruit ~

I understand love,
the flames of passion.
A splendid ride on
a towering wave,
the love it takes to make
a child tender and sweet.

I've never felt the flames
of passion,
or had a fire of my own.
My sky is empty,
the birds are dying.
My heart is a shriveled pit
of some forgotten fruit.

My mask is always smiling
as I struggle every day.
Meanwhile, the sparrows
are dropping from the sky,
their tiny corpses,
reflections of my heart.

~ I the Tie ~

I, the tie

am the power point,

the signature of you.

A bow atop

the finely wrapped gift,

the bow that ties it all together.

A splash of color

that tells the tale of you,

unique, its silent voice,

that tells your story, your signature.

The explanation point of your character woven into silk,

the threads of life.

I so love being a tie.

I do so much more than just hang around,

I the tie am a statement.

You can dress me up,

dress me down,

take me anywhere.

I am the silent voice

your partner, your best friend,

hanging out for the day.

I am the skin in the game

and the Windsor Knot of perfection.

I am the wow, the pow
tied lovingly by hands that care,
hands that share.
So proudly the elegance of you.

~ January 2013 ~

Here we are again, our footsteps slowly walking
upon desolation road.
Window watching, I seem to do a lot of that this time of year.
When outside is so temporary, a snowy bridge
from one warm room to the next.

It's a popular time for crows.
I see them everywhere, soaring from limb to limb;
my beloved regal, winter soldiers.
It's a time of snow white skin, heavy coats, hats and
gloves and always my favorite scarf.
It's white and soft, warm and thick when it surrounds me.
I love to burrow into it.

It's January and the days are getting longer
but the roads still high with snow.
The sun far away, a stranger still.
I so yearn for it to descend to feel the fellowship of
this blazing ornament that decorates the sky.

So what should I do? How should I survive? My body's core
chilled to the bone but I've been through this before.
My spirit on autopilot, as I lay undercover and wait.

In January the door of hope is slightly ajar. The hands of winter still holding tight as I wait so patiently, wait for that first new bud on the naked branch to blossom.

~ My Body's Death ~

I have no memory of my body's death

when my hands flew away, unusable wings.

My legs, misplaced water waves, that cannot walk

and the permanent night of a sightless ocean,

where blind words have no voice.

My body is a new house,

haunted with ghosts who remember.

~ My Brothers ~

This day, the sky painted white with the richness of clouds,
a mural of soft brush strokes. I thrill to the
sound of your battle cry.

My beloved crows, I hear you calling, loud and raucous
in April's sky. Ebony musicians, I love your every note,
harmonizing with the choir of all birds.

My brothers, I love your confidence, never afraid to be heard.
Little generals, commanding land and sky
with a dominant air.

In all seasons, you remain permanent dwellers,
forever loyal to earth and sky, surveying the land
from your post in the birch, the maple, the elm.

I love everything about you, dear brothers,
the intensity of your soul,
a sentinel perched in the highest branches,
an icon of all seasons.

Noble guardian, the echo of your call can be heard across the
world, and forever in my own backyard.

~ My Voice ~

Silent was my voice,

stepping backwards

before I found myself.

When I was very young

I was a bird without a song,

trampled feathers.

The cloth to polish my shine,

never woven.

Cruel words,

the voices always taunting my spirit.

Tangled in sharp wires was my cage,

for years always a veil to mask my pain.

And so I flew away,

but the sky was the same.

Flying in circles, defeated was my soul.

Upon that last day,

my footsteps would never touch the ground.

Stolen was my life, my freedom,

my tattered song hushed and bruised.

But God was with me,

the stream of moonlight

upon this darkened street.

From the sentence of death, He saved me.

In His beloved arms,

five weeks I slept,

unheard and unmoving.

Until the compassion of our Lord

sent me down an altered path.

A place of grace, where my aura

was brighter.

Today I am a bird,

though my wings are broken,

at last I have found my voice to sing.

~ Outside the Shadows ~

The shield slides up,

surrounding, protecting.

Guarding hurtful feelings,

shyness and overwhelming

obstacles, never conquered.

The shield is a friend,

an enemy,

which has existed forever.

It slides down at night,

allowing sleep to prevail.

Sometimes on awakening,

it is forgotten,

but only for a moment.

Then it slides into place,

locked securely for the day.

Can it be unlocked, let down,

enabling happiness?

Somewhere deep within

the confines of the mind,

the key will be found,

allowing hope

to walk outside the shadows.

~ Searching ~

I would like to hold the sky

gently in my arms and feel

the falcon in my soul.

I want to feel someone next to me,

but the shadows are always silent.

My face in the mirror is darkness.

Spider legs of fear have chased

away my dreams. I have been alone

so long, my shell is thick.

I want to get off this lost road,

this bare earth.

In the thunder it is raining stones,

sky and earth are lovers always.

Where is my lover?

Who will love ME?

~ September; The Final Ballad ~

Blue sky, it seems a shade darker in September,

the hue a little heavier. I don't know why.

I do know, this moment, a hawk flew by.

I heard his piercing battle cry,

lifting my heart to the clouds

where he reigns...

Now I am a cloud,

my spirit euphoric, drifting here.

Pure white is my complexion,

delicious as whip cream.

And now I am the wind,

warm and gentle.

My countenance peaceful,

sweet as angel's breath.

I the wind, so thrilled to be alive

the stream of my existence,

frolicking through the trees.

Now I am the leaves,

rustling in the breeze.

Mighty maple, my home

the branch where I thrive,

a place from which foliage does fall,

a canopy for crickets.

And now I am the cricket,

the door of my duration quickly closing.

My song a tranquil lullaby

in the air of summer, very soon,

very soon to be silenced.

At last I am the cicadas,

my ghostly presence, a fading light.

Heartbreaking is my ballad,

in these final September hours.....

In November's home,
a single lit candle, one loyal flame,
quiets my soul.

And here come chickadees,
sparrows and juncos,
adorning autumn's sky
with their wings full of blessings.

I am grateful, grateful for God's tender grace,
this miracle that is our life.

~ Summer Dreams ~

The sunrise is when the dream begins,

awakening everything beautiful.

When summer arrives,

an eternal smile in my heart.

Summer, my best friend,

sunshine, my greatest ally

brings to my soul warmth, peace and happiness.

Every moment we're together, romancing the sun

my heart and soul, overflowing with serenity.

The warmth of the day opens my spirit to a treasure of dreams,

I adore everything of this season.

The birds and the bees, the flowers and the sky.

The sun in my heart, a nest of dreams

where even the ridiculous can happen.

I am standing, tall as the trees,

my arms outstretched in bliss,

beckoning a butterfly to grace me with her beauty.

Let us not forget my beloved crickets,

serenading my soul with a steady cadence

of their beloved heart songs,

all day, from morning through night.

One of my favorite things to observe,

the blossoming of a flower.

Summer, sweet summer,

you are the radiance of my heart,

you bring the blush of roses to my cheeks.

Summer, my beloved,

you are everything dreams are made of.

The brilliance of each hour

so breathtaking it cannot stand still,

runs away on fast sneakers.

When the sun goes down,

oh how the moon does rise.

The depth of its soul, mysterious and resplendent,

in the evening shadows of the night,

the constellations, a gift from God.

The stars, the stars, the brilliance of the stars

brings light to the darkness,

thank you, Lord, for everything.

~ The Other Side of the Cross ~

Loneliness and fear are vanishing
as we follow the light from above,
I feel His gentle arms surround me
God's most sacred, healing love.

Unto my life I'm given
a new and powerful lease,
my heart is overflowing
calm waves of genuine peace.

The wind here scented with roses
in this garden of breathtaking wings,
I feel the grace of euphoria
when I hear the angels sing.

Always here in this field of dreams
the miracle of youth deep within,
the purity of the heavens
the warmth of a beloved friend.

Whatever your favorite time of day
the dawn of early morn,
or the twilight shadows of evening
when the moon and stars are born.

In this meadow of paradise
an eternity of radiance exudes,
in every beautiful spirit
this peaceful, alluring view.

He died for the sins of mankind
a grave and unforgettable loss,
carrying His light to the heavens
from the other side of the cross.

~ A Much Needed Prayer ~

It can be a fatal game,

when the lie within the needle is laced with venom.

What is this madness,

every day teetering on the plank above shark-filled waters?

Always caught in this vicious cycle,

needing to seek the door of salvation.

You have to ask yourself this question,

which finish line will you cross?

One has a stone with your name on it,

the other will be crossed if only upon your knees,

you say a prayer and listen to the message of God.

Always the voice of compassion,

begging you to drop the needle.

When does the battle end,

it ends when the Holy Voice whispers in your ear.

~ Circle of Heavenly Light ~

He rises each morning at dawn, tasting the ecstasy of the fading
night,
to be handed working tools,
to toil lovingly each day at familiar tasks,
to feel the grain, the wood in his weathered hands.

The groove of a lifetime, holding one tool or another,
so rewarding, this labor--not tedious,
fulfilling a lifetime of pure peace and noble deeds.

Home at last to hold his newborn in his arms,
to breathe the fragrance of innocence,
to see his child smile,
to feel the tender kiss of his wife, her soft lips upon his own,
to watch a lifetime of sunsets grow old.

Beneath the moon and stars--never afraid,
faith is the song in their hearts,
the harmony of growing wise together.

One winter night the light slipped away softly, sweetly,
without a whisper of fear,
awakening the youth, the strength of purity,
an incredible feeling of peace.

All around him the softness of arms, and the strength of hope,
love flowing like the warmest, the sweetest of rivers, through his
blood,
encircled in the brightest of lights, utter happiness
igniting,
his heart,
his soul,
his spirit.
Home at last, encircled in God's most radiant light,
the warmth of God's eternal love.

~ Embroidered Thoughts ~

Embroidered thoughts of the mind are what
flowers are to a garden.

Poems that blossom with grandeur,
the birth of a vision in the writer's mind.

Oh for the love of poetry,
take my hand, let's dance.
Oh for the love of poetry,
so precious, as each thought a beloved child
I devote myself to.

We are partners for life.
The thrill, the pride,
the creation of you,
my wings.

Oh gracious Lord,
I give thanks to you for my imagination,
the contentment of creating,
and the pedestal it brings me to.

The beauty of these words are
the vibrant threads of
embroidered thoughts.....

~ Fear ~

The sun is shining
as icy rain pours from clouds.
No one can see the fear
dancing in her heart.

The sparrows are cold,
their song frozen in the hallway.

Today, her space is narrow.
This moment,
when the ice rain pours in,
nightmares are real.

The face in the mirror is a grimace,
a monster.
She feels the shark's marble eyes,
the razor fins beneath the cold.

The sun is a yellow dragon,
a serpent's tail.
The black tongue
flickers at the fire.

There are seeds beneath the fire,
a tiny garden in the backyard,
a place for hope to blossom.

~ Bitter Lemons ~

On good days the paralyzed smile at
people who are walking, the sun is a
yellow bird in the sky. Their broken spines
are flowers on these days.

When the storm marches through,
the canary dies, they have swallowed
all the lemons and feel the sharp edge
of bitter wind.

The fish are frozen in their small, glass world.
Dark rises, while sheets of hornets sting
from their wild nest of rage!!!

~ *How the Candle Flickers* ~

I walk to the edge of shore. My foot

dips timidly to water. My heart shrinks

and swells with the crystal tide. Always

anticipation, that ripple of fear before

plunging in. Overhead, a ballet, gulls

gliding, white-winged angels in the salty mist.

Effortless, a writer's dream to soar. Oh, the

sunrise of poetry, reborn again and again,

the infant crowning above waves.

Ask the wind, the wave, a star, a bird,

what courage it takes to soar.

Darkness drips wax into wings

of flame. What blindfold shall I wear to

follow my dream?

~ My Heaven ~

Beyond the sun, the stars, the moon, my heaven.
The birth of flowers, never born.
A new ocean, where the waves are pink,
its excited heart beating like His kiss,
tender and soft, trembles against our lips.

A paradise, the strength of trees growing
tall, taller still. A harmony beyond
what can be imagined.
A softer tide, a ripple of waves,
the pulse of every blossom, the melody of love.
Angelic scent of the sweetest flowers.

A unicorn as if in prayer,
head bowed nibbling grass.
Overhead in a cloudless sky,
angels soaring in a gentle breeze.

In the still-blue sky, the sun a golden fire
now, in shadows slowly simmers.
Evening, a black rose, dark petals of silk,
slowly blossoms.
Painting stars, God sighs, smiles,
lays down His brush, not yet dry.

~ All My Little Critters ~

It's mid-May and the sun has finally fallen,
a cool breeze chatting with the magnificent greenery of these
lofty trees.
Upon the boughs and in the skies angels singing,
sparrow, robin, junco, so dazzling.
A cardinal, berry-red, perched on a branch of maple,
my heart delights when I hear the voice of his song.
The season still too young for the symphony of cicadas.
My very precious crickets, right on cue with their fascinating
harmony that can only be them,
serenading all those who care to listen.
So many spirits seduced by these exquisite entertainers.
At last the sun is finally sleeping, tucked comfortably away in its
evening suite
waiting to arouse and carry its perfect light,
to extend God's calling, to shine upon the world again.
The baritone tree frogs fill the darkness with their unique and
raspy melody.
In the divinity of dawn, the air becomes silent as the night
critters sleep before the early bird's first notes. That one eager
bird with this day's first song.
And God, of course, is always watching, spreading His wings of
love for all to feel
throughout yet another day's divine awakening.

~ *Summer* ~

I have suffered the atrocity of sunsets,

overwhelmed by this dichotomy.

My heart, the stem of the lavender flower, broken.

You are a yellow balloon, a blowfish puffed up,

kept alive by love's helium.

I may be presumptuous, but sometimes I feel

mine, mine are the only hands, the tender hands to

keep you from falling, falling from the scaffold

in the sky. Standing at the altar, weeping, I hear

the organ's music, but the services have not yet begun.

~ Moccasins ~

Ahead of me, my feet always running,

I place no blame,

but the shadow of myself

never far behind.

The day it happened, the sky

choked with tears. Always that

tired road worn from traveling.

I shall tread it no longer,

they walk softly now,

these moccasins above the ground.

~ Wax Museum ~

And so it begins, the ladder leaning against the barn.

A fresh coat of paint, incandescent light, look what you've done,
wardens with your ruined sentence of love.

I know you can't help your weakness,

the sorrow tucked deep in my pocket, soil from the grave, teeth
seal the zipper, rusted by the flood of my own tears.

In the death chamber, the maiden sleeps in casting shadows....
ALONE.

~ Rag Doll Smile ~

It never wavers, one you can count on.

Fluttering memories of innocence jumping rope

through rainbows, through hoops.

Gazing at the world through eyes of serenity.

The first moon landing, the first step a toddler takes,

that grin that enriches your heart.

Time passing, evolution, a galaxy of stars lighting up the world.

I look at the smile on my rag doll's face,

it touches my heart.

A paradise of reminiscence, peaceful joy,

a genuine collection of fabric and dreams, sacred memories.

~ Olive Branch ~

Imagine a place of paradise,

where fear does not exist.

Everywhere, angels

and their delicate hands,

holding an olive branch.

Every day, the world is born again,

with the rising of the sun.

From the voice of birds,

their sweet harmony,

promoting peace.

Let every heart be fearless

and the love of God be in every heart.

When the golden light appears,

every morning sings,

a new miracle.

We are blessed with the gifts

of another dawn awakening

and the rising of

the peaceful, brilliant sun.

~ Before the Window ~

It feels like I have been waiting a lifetime for you,

my heart full of dreams, not yet broken.

Not yet broken from the years when the moon was small,

do you know how hard it was to look into nothing?

Deaf from all sounds,

the stillness of being blind.

And now the day is approaching for you to arrive,

but today, in this moment a space in the wall.

So many dreams have died here in my heart while waiting,

only a patch to cover your gaping eye.

At the window,

for months we have been expecting.

At last you have arrived,

one glorious eye open.

More than a window,

a dream long awaited.

A nest of treasures where hope lives,

true love approaching, a paradise is

here now.

A new view opening wings to my heart,

always the roses more precious than rubies at the window.

~ Single Black Rose ~

Cold rain, cold, cold rain
in the summer's sky,
only ice water running through the stream.

Shoes now too small,
so much anguish.

The balance beam no longer.

Falling, falling
from the tightrope of lost dreams
in the blackest of nights.

My soul, a broken top,
spinning out of control
riddled with fear.

There's a fire in the distant trees
and an old dented pot,
boiling over with the anger of my muted screams.

Time, time
is everywhere and nowhere.
Flies hovering above my head
in this tornado of wasted hours.

Time standing still,
why is it still standing?

Blackest of rose petals,
razor sharp tips.
Frozen in my bleeding heart,
ropes pulled so tight.

~ Not Through Rose-Colored Glasses ~

I can hold my head up,

it feels wonderful to look at the sky,

when I'm writing, when I'm writing, when I'm writing.

I fly, I soar.

When I walked, I was a bird with broken wings,

now I'm in a chair and my wings open up

and I soar higher than I could ever walk, than I could ever dream.

All those miles have vanished beneath my feet.

There's a crow on the fence

just looking at me,

I look at him, I look at him, I look at him,

and we are one.

My soul is deeper than it ever was, deep rivers amaze me,

I'm stolen away by the glory and beauty of water.

I'll never forget how the ground felt beneath my feet,

it's ok, it's ok, it's ok.

When I write poetry, my spirit soars in the sky,

it grabs hold of my dreams and I'm flying.

I was having a little writer's block,

my heart was weeping and the sky was black,

then I listened to the music of Sam Baker,

and once again I soared.

Sometimes fear curls up like a broken web,

and I am the spider without any legs.

~ Nobody but You ~

Nobody but you

can fix my broken wings,

nobody but you can teach a bird to sing.

When the moon and stars align at night

it's you who painted this heavenly sight.

Thank you, Lord, for the aura that you bring.

Nobody but you

can make the ocean roar,

nobody but you can let the eagle soar.

The sun rises to dawn another day

illuminating the blazing, golden rays.

The waves dance and rush to kiss the shore.

Waiting in the shadows

when all hope has disappeared,

I hear your voice calling me

so gentle and so clear.

Nobody but you

can make the world unite,

nobody but you can hold the shining light.

When our dreams feel eternally lost

we think of your Son who died upon the cross.

We'll say a pray as day drifts into night.

~ Lily ~

In the bedroom of spring, the infant wakes,
newborn buds smiling everywhere
and God graced us with the lily,
a flower from the heavens, so elegant.

Listen intently to the robin's song,
to the sparrows and bluebirds.
Listen deeply to the music of wind
and you just might hear a prayer without words.
Hear the lilacs whisper their quiet song,
born in the meadow of spring.

~ Winter's Sunset ~

All day, her heart

crinkled and brown,

blood of the winter rose

achingly tender, hard and brash.

She skates on thin ice, of blue air

in cold wind, her dress,

blowing a lavender fire.

The music of winter

stirs the dance faster,

performing for the soul of one

and those who watched its quick descent.

Singing on the wings of reincarnation

life and death forever,

makes one sweet song.

~ Death Is not Real ~

Death is not real, it is a faraway phantom.

I lay in the tranquility of shadows, not a casket,

but a purple sunset.

I'm not afraid to die,

death is not real.

My heart blossoms like a velvet rose,

beating like the wings of a bee.

Autumn is approaching, like a candle.

Its flame snuffed out by winter,

white as bed sheets, winter, white as the ivory moon.

Poems are like snowflakes, no two are alike,

all night the angels are falling, silencing the darkness.

Death is not real, it is a faraway phantom.

~ Words ~

On good days when the river is high, I set my pen to paper.

The hive of the mind always buzzing

as the kettle of thoughts begins to whistle.

So excited are these wings to soar,

this script of words writing themselves across the sky

and when the river is dry,

a good writer knows.

Just wait a moment or two for the buds in paradise to be inspired,

for the garden of thoughts to blossom.

Ah, so sweet are the pungent flowers,

the sweetest heaven,

the gateway of another world.

Poetry the harmony of wind,

travels though me, such precious jewels to polish and shine.

They take me away on the string of a kite,

my spirit, my heart and soul soaring higher, higher still,

on the harmonious wings of my imagination.

~ Writing Angels ~

There's a paradise in my mind,
when thoughts are lit by stars.

Hearts excited, kicking up their heels,
dazzling the night's sky.

The lion roars in jubilation,
my heart filled with pride,
as angels whisper thoughts to me
in passionate voices.

My spirit dances,
as words flow easily
from the river of my mind.

I'm showered in rose petals,
my spirit flourishes with so much joy
my heart cannot bear it.

My soul now calm, my purest,
wildest thoughts are yours,
my darling, my love—my poems.

Until the ink dries
and the last passionate thought
trembles humbly from my pen.

~ Lost and Found ~

"Mind my life," I heard a voice,

unknown and searching for a home.

My soul was like the open pages

of fine poetry, delicate, sensitive.

So I floated to the clouds,

hiding in the trees.

The crows would watch

and talk amongst themselves.

I was unseen, so I stayed.

I would hear their voices

down below calling my name.

I could see their eyes unleashed

and endlessly hungry.

I was unable to find my voice

. . . . .and I cried.

I disappeared for many years

and walked alone.

The street was hard, the corners sharp.

I became the crow, soaring high.

My eyes were dark and full of thunder,

two bolts of lightning gone to sleep.

When I woke up, my legs were gone,

but through the fire, I found my voice.

~ Hidden Beauty ~

Black crows circle.

Serpent's tongue flickers at the ashes of a child's heart,

thoughts and fears of yesteryear closing in.

Kisses blown into the wind.

Dreams escape into a place, I don't know where,

people, places, nameless faces, adding to the pain.

Soaring through the clouds.

Strength, a foreign word, becoming real,

days reflect and interact with the hidden beauty of a soul.

A ray of sun touches my shoulder.

The embodiment of fear now chased away,

casting shadows in the graveyard of yesterday.

~ November's Grave ~

Leaves dead on the ground

defeated soldiers,

but the war has just begun.

Days seem to us, less brief,

arms of men and women

bare and cold.

Wind shrills through the oak,

frail twigs, slender.

I talk to their shadows,

shadows of crows talk back,

tramps of the grey skies

with harmonica voices.

If the legless dancers fall,

mute in their white skirt,

an early snow.

~ Ghost ~

Wilted iris, polished lid
no resting place to die,
resurrected, tormented memories
sleep-deprived, what's inside?

Sharp antique blades, juggling fear
attic walls are breathing,
floorboards constant screaming
and the ancient ghost is rocking in her chair.

This mind's a tortured chamber of strength
that's lost inside of me,
puppets dangling on strings
laughter echoes madly.

Children teaching cruelty
wounds that are reopened,
cattle prods poking
branding irons smoking.

The scarlet letter "S" scalded in her mind
icy blue roads impossible,
and the memories of yesterday, awake
the angel of compassion eliminates the power of despair.

A tombstone in the earth
her name, at last written there,
she's running in the shadows
of haunted, frightened trees and slips
on old leaves of the fall.

In the cemetery she is walking
a child's voice keeps talking,
until she eventually sees the writing on the wall
the demon's rope inside her head,
winds that were insane.

The knots are finally loosening
ridding her of all the pain,
the ghost that was kept alive
now buried in the blizzard of her fear.

~ Apple Slices ~

This world is a sphere of cement,

cracked and fragile.

The wave of evolution slipped

us to the shore,

a hamburger sizzling on the grill,

a slice of apple,

the garden's sweet temptation.

~ At Last a Dream Come True ~

Pastor Jack drove past that old barn

so many times each day,

then an idea came to him,

"Let's make it a chapel to pray."

Ten years flew by so quickly

but it was still just a thought,

then God whispered in Jack's ear,

something he never forgot.

"You can remodel that barn

with the aid of many people

and perhaps on top of that structure,

someone could build a glorious steeple."

Workers came from miles around

everyone lending a hand,

this was not just a barn anymore,

it became a chapel, a chapel so grand.

Pastor Jack's vision came true

a place of worship bringing a smile to the Lord,

as He watched people sing and pray,

all together in one accord.

~ City Streets ~

The city drags itself awake in weary air.

My footsteps drag on crowded streets.

Heat rises in waves and shimmers on a sea of

cars moving like turtles. Thoughts of home.

A dream mirage of faces, hard sobs shaking me apart.

A cacophony of blaring horns and city sounds.

Feeling very small, squinting at the window glass

and buildings tall, reaching for the sky.

Daylight slips away. Pizza smells linger in the air,

and no one cares. Running back and forth

between the outstretched arms of darkness,

an inkwell of black spills across the sky.

~ In Her Dream She Cried ~

Shadow hands nudged her

wheelchair into the room.

It rolled against her bed

with a soft thud,

and in her dream she cried.

Purple-black thunder heads

rushed across the sky,

lightning flashed,

leaving a scent of copper,

like pennies fast-fried.

In the broken light,

her black chair resembled

a headless ghost,

and in her dream she cried.

Lightning flashed again

illuminating the vision of her life,

forever a web of interlacing,

silken threads tying the knots of anguish.

~ The Ivory Glove ~

I keep my lonely vigil, watching him die,

a skeleton wrapped in ghost-white sheets.

I fall into his sunken eyes.

"Stay where you are," the angel bride said,

and motioned with her ivory glove.

He felt the soft kiss of darkness

and opened his arms to embrace a land of doves.

"Stay where you are," the angel bride said to me,

and looked into my soul.

I'm in a silent place of pain,

the only sound, crows gathering

on a crooked branch.

I stand by the graveside, his name etched in stone

and watch white feathers drifting in the breeze,

or perhaps it was an ivory glove.

~ Jewels of Winter ~

A single cardinal glides above

a meadow of bright eyes, blinking.

Contemplate the beauty of the earth,

the jewels of winter. Step into the

grand ballroom. The cold air

visits your neck and shakes the trees

of crystal chimes. Listen to the quiet of the

snow-covered floor, the only music,

the wind and birds that have stayed. Breaking

the silence, until the symphony of spring

awakens the world.

~ Tropical Fish ~

Imagine a universe beneath the sea,

all people tropical fish.

Every day a holiday,

little bodies ornately wrapped.

Kings and queens, prince and princesses,

ruling this kingdom from coral castles.

A gift from God, these aquatic angels,

their spirits a rainbow of serenity.

Professional swimmers, gliding deep beneath the water,

liberal spirits, tiny little fins dancing.

Even within a shimmering glass world, currents of water,

their only blood.

A peaceful nation, living within a wave of harmony . . ..

~ Crows of Late Autumn ~

Outside inhaling autumn's sweet scent,

rustic.....inviting.

Sunlight shimmering through a lacy

curtain of clouds.

It's October. I'm content in

the cozy shadows of this

comfortable den. Overhead, the

horizon, irresistible as always.

I never met a sunset I have

not fallen completely in love with.

This day's sky, gift-wrapped in

the finest of cloth. White clouds

of sheer satin bliss.

Perched in a tree, a guardian,

a presence in black.

My beloved crow. His voice

greeting me with confident laughter.

Fingers of a chilly wind

strumming the chimes as the

strong breeze rustles through the leaves.

131

~ Full Circle ~

Oh trees standing before me, beautiful, silent, tall sentinels.

I've always felt connected to you. You're a twist of oaken arms,

each season more beautiful than the next.

Your birth in spring, verdant,

infant buds growing more breathtaking every moment.

Summer, your leaves green flags, excited hands

waving in the wind.

Wind, my labor in autumn, when a drop of my blood is Picasso's

brush painting barn doors rusty and red.

Winter stands regal, adorned

in silver gowns, floating for eternity on glass bottom boats.

And the infantry standing brave, barefoot in the cold.

Shoulder to shoulder, this tireless war. Their naked heads

thrown back towards the sky.

Watching, waiting, listening for

the womb to open, for that one forgotten cry.

Fallen soldiers red, yellow, gold, copper

somberly drifting in our little pond.

And always the harmonious crows.

Their magical voices calling my name.

~ Cold Beauty ~

Dark sky of night in winter,

the wind a haunting ballad,

the notes are cold.

A wild breeze through long arms of trees,

posed like phantoms in moonlit gloom.

Slick with crystal chimes, the branches sleep in

frozen tombs of ice, heavy laden, bowing low,

waiting for the next curtain call

when the wind and sky bring snowflakes

to adorn the trees with stars.

Inch by inch, mountains form.

Beyond the midnight hour

an eastern light sparkles,

diamond mines on mountain snow.

~ Sylvia ~

There is a heart beating on my sleeve.

No cover to hide anxious eyes.

A sparrow trapped within a cage.

I know the bottom, I have gone down fighting,

perished, drifted up. Dead eyes stare into the grave's reflection.

My soul barely floating, barely feeling, ecstatic drowning,

déjà vu and there she comes again, plunging, darting.

The vampire's fangs, rabid bats, gnarled fur.

Wrapped in its night shawl, shadow of the angel's wings

and always, that hammer pounding.

I feel the needle's sharp points and the wound reopened.

The song of my plague, as the turntable skips relentlessly.

She sits, detached, drinking shots of venom, the ghost inside of me.

~ In the Flame of a Summer's Dream ~

What is that sound I hear?
The question posed by many,
answered wrongly by many more!

The song you hear, my precious cicadas.
The ballad of a summer dream
felt deeply, harmoniously in the leafy branches of my own heart,
as I gaze overhead at drifting clouds.
The musical continues...

They are the great musicians performing oh so contently on
summer's stage.
Hiding among trees,
coiled in leafy branches.
Holding themselves in high esteem for
they know their hearts are filled with wonder,
their exquisite song, so beautiful.

The last ballad written,
the signature of this most enchanting season,
their incessant hum quite mesmerizing.
They are the emperors of this gala time of year.
Maybe that is why all who listen call them the unseen ghosts of
summer.

Intoxicated is my spirit.
Always my beloved, amazing musicians,
I adore you!
In the hour of twilight I hear your song
harmonizing the world.
I'm listening my darlings,
as you're serenading with crickets in the eyes of moonlight,
until the last star fades slowly at dawn.

~Winter's Stage ~

I am listening to the whispers of the season,
the dark and delicate whispers as the last
leaf falls from October's grip.
And I hear autumn ride away in the rusty wagon
overflowing with orange and copper leaves.

I imagine the echo of a galloping horse
through forests of bare-naked trees.
Mother Nature sits back for a moment
and takes a short breath before the next act begins.

It has been predicted, the snow,
on every channel.
We go to the window and gaze skyward
waiting for the miracle to appear.

Through December's hazel eyes,
looking out for her children,
the first flakes begin to dance from the ceiling of slate.

And from the heavens,
crystals of pure white blossoms
ever so silently twirl like
graceful ballerinas on winter's stage.

~ Faith is the Answer ~

What do God and angels think about

when they look down upon the world?

The sun is shining and butterflies are floating to the music of
birds, tomorrow it could rain.

Seconds can be many days for a family without food.

A lifetime is not long enough to hold our love.

Their daughter may perish without a bone marrow transplant,

her ballet slippers buried in the ground.

Will she be dancing in heaven?

So many questions,

I believe faith is the answer.

What do God and angels think about when they

look down upon the world?

If they looked through my window today, they would find me
smiling, soaring on wings of poetry.

The sun is shining and butterflies are floating to the music of
birds, tomorrow it could rain.

~ A Perfect Summer Day ~

Draw me the picture of a perfect summer day
and I'll give you the horizon,
a horizon of dreams.

Feel this day's wind, its gentle caress,
and I will give you the birds, ecstatically serenading.
God's harmony, a perfect melody of angels singing.

If I give you clouds,
will you give me their purity?
Broad shoulders of heavenly mountains,
my heart a peaceful drum,
joyfully beating along with nature's exquisite
performance upon center stage.

This poem cannot be complete
nor any poems of the summer.
My spirit held hostage in the sun's embrace,
freedom sashaying like long flowing skirts.
The voice of many birds,
carrying their delightful song
upon the wings of twilight.

~ Risen From the Ashes ~

Sixteen years old

and the road was dark.

Bullets shooting from the mouths of classmates

injured my soul and left me feeling worthless.

Depression, anxiety and fear,

my self-esteem wounded badly.

From my heart and soul,

I heard God's voice.

"You are worthy, follow me my child."

Always seeking brighter tomorrows,

the door to college now open.

In a single moment,

the dark clouds departed, euphoria lifted my soul.

Turning twenty six years old,

I walked a path lined with roses.

But in the haunting shadows, a desperate addict lurking,

only innocence flowing through my veins.

A vicious blow stopped the hands of time,

no sun or moon, only darkness lay in my wake.

Death stealing my last few breaths of life,

but the hand of God pulled me up, I rejoiced.

With His love, I have "Risen From the Ashes."

~ Invincible ~

I remember when

I read into the night,

my own hand held a fork to eat

and a pen to write.

I thought I was invincible.

I remember when

I was very shy,

needing to escape

so I could reach the sky.

I thought I was invincible.

My wheelchair's in the corner

my aide's a little late,

I listen to the birds outside

I lay in bed and wait.

I know I'm not invincible.

Today my sight is damaged

I cannot see to read,

I have the help of other hands

for everything I need.

I know I'm not invincible.

This message is for everyone

be careful what you do,

life is very precious

a gift God gave to you.

Don't think that you're invincible.

Made in the USA
Middletown, DE
21 December 2021

54551801R00084